Harris and the Pines

Harris and the Pines

by RICHARD H. UTT

PACIFIC PRESS PUBLISHING ASSOCIATION

MOUNTAIN VIEW, CALIFORNIA   OMAHA, NEBRASKA

THIS BRIEF STORY HAS BEEN WRITTEN BECAUSE—

First, as most of its customers and friends know, Harris Pine Mills is a church-owned industry. Many people refer to the company as "the church" and do so out of sincerity and respect. How, they ask, did the Mills become the property of a church, and how does this affect company policies and operations?

Second, Harris Pine Mills is also of interest because it is not merely a sawmill, but an integrated industry. It operates tree farms and builds and maintains roads. It fells timber, hauls the logs with its own truck fleets, and operates sawmills. It seasons, surfaces, and manufactures lumber, and then produces furniture, finished and unfinished, and sells the product.

Another aspect of the Mills which deserves to be better known is that special attention is given to providing young men and women with employment to help pay their way through college. When these students graduate, some accept calls to serve in schools and hospitals in Asia, Africa, Latin America, and the islands of the sea, in what amounts to a private "Peace Corps" sponsored by their denomination. Thus, the company's influence extends far beyond Pendleton, Oregon, to the remotest part of the globe.

Finally, this is the story of a man who has added another chapter to the story of the "American dream"; who wanted to enter a business with no blind alleys, no upper limits to growth and success; who, by dint of hard work, ingenuity, and trust in God, achieved far more than he had hoped to achieve.

The Author.

Contents

Clyde Harris at the age of eight.

A Businessman Is Born

The iron horse chuffed slowly into the Union Pacific station at Walla Walla, Washington, belching black smoke from its tall, funneled stack. With a screeching of brakes, a hissing of steam, and a clanging of bells, the engine ground to a halt and its string of wooden coaches began to disgorge weary, bone-sore passengers arriving from points east.

Among those alighting from the train that blustery, teeth-chattering day in February, 1886, were James and Bertha Harris, from Waupun, Wisconsin, with their six children, George, Myrtle, Mattie, Clarence, Jim, and Darrell. George, the oldest, was sixteen; the other five stairstepped down to Darrell, aged two.

Before migrating westward, Harris had been a jockey, done carpenter work, and traveled between Kansas City and Chicago as a merchandise broker. Finally he had nailed together a new saloon in Waupun and stocked it well with the product of the brewer's and distiller's arts. However, the night before his saloon was to open, an arsonist had reduced the uninsured enterprise to charcoal and cinders. Then, only a few days later, the Harris home also caught fire and burned to the ground. The family escaped, but saved few of their possessions.

Staggering from this double blow, Harris decided to migrate westward and build a new life for his family, as thousands of others were doing. Besides, he had health problems, and his doctor advised him to seek employment in the drier climate of the West.

Arriving in Walla Walla, the family hired a wagon and team and jogged along a rutted road to Milton, Oregon, eleven miles to the south. Here James Harris found promise of employment as a carpenter and decided to stay. He rented an acre of land in the outskirts and built a four-room frame house on it.

Milton, Umatilla County, lies in the Walla Walla River Valley, an area whose rich soil produces wheat, peas, and many kinds of fruit: peaches, plums, apples, cherries, apricots, and berries. Prime cattle and sheep country stretches away toward the horizon on every side, and on the nearby Wallowa and Green Mountains grow forests of pine and spruce.

The area's first settler had built a log cabin there in 1856. During the next three decades several hundreds of families took up land in the vicinity, so that by 1874 the settlement had grown to sufficient size to warrant a post office. In 1886, the year the Harris family arrived, Milton received its charter and became an incorporated town.

During the Harrises' first seven years in Milton three more children joined the family—Claude, Clyde, and Hazel. Clyde, eighth of the nine, was born March 9, 1890.

One of Clyde's earliest memories is of the treeless lot shimmering under the parching rays of the midsummer sun. Over the stark landscape only one patch of shade could be found, aside from such small shadows as those of the pump and the outhouse, and that was in the shelter of the house itself. In this spot of comparative coolness a passel of small fry, including the three youngest Harrises, gathered to chatter, play tag and follow-the-leader, and quarrel.

During their early childhood Clyde and Claude usually wore disintegrating overalls and shirts handed down from older brothers, while a faded calico dress, plus a hand-sewn undergarment, more or less covered the portions of baby Hazel that they were designed to cover. During the warmer part of the year the children went barefoot. But, what matter? Only a few of the tots who congregated from neighboring homes sported more extravagant attire than they. Hardship was the way of life for pioneer families, in most cases more liberally endowed with children than with finances.

Still, life was something to enjoy, especially for the children too small to realize they were underprivileged. Life meant roaming the hills behind the house, picking wild flowers in the spring, chasing cows, snaring squirrels, sleeping soundly at night, and eating heartily at mealtime—at least on those occasions when the Harris table provided enough food for two adults and all the ravenous children.

Home revolved around the kitchen, the largest room in the house, where Mother Harris, a thin, somewhat frail, deeply religious woman, presided. Here, with the help of the older girls, she baked wheat bread and corn bread, boiled potatoes, cabbage, beans, and carrots, and canned pears and applesauce. Here the girls churned the cream, making butter for the family to use and to sell.

Somehow, along with managing the large household, Mrs. Harris found time and strength to take in washing from some of the more prosperous townspeople, thus supplementing her husband's meager income. She liked nice things in the home and, through industry and thrift, managed to secure a few of them—a lounge, mattress, center table, chairs, dishes, and silverware.

When Clyde was a little fellow, his mother would catch him up on her lap and talk to him about Jesus and about being a good boy. But he would soon wiggle away from her and go off and play. One of the things his mother impressed upon him was the need for being honest and straightforward. She would never tell an untruth even in a joking way. If his brothers or sisters told him something false, even in fun, he would turn to his mother and ask, "Mother, is that so?"

"That is what they say," she would gravely reply, and Clyde knew he should not believe it. Such was the influence of Mother Harris that eventually all the children but one accepted her religion.

Father Harris, an average-sized man with sideburns and whiskers, was a veteran of the Civil War. He worked as a carpenter to support his family, but was hampered by chronic ill health. Though he gambled some, he was otherwise a frugal man who would pick up a stray bolt, washer, or nail he found on the ground and later deposit it in a box where he kept such things. During the recession of the mid-1890's he worked summers for fifty cents a day.

In 1895 Clyde's father, as a war veteran, received a $500 bonus check from the Government. With $350 of this sudden wealth, he bought an acre of fruitful land by the Walla Walla River, with a small house and a large barn on it. To Clyde, this place was a little paradise. Bordering it on three sides were cottonwoods and willows. The acre had apple, prune, pear, and cherry trees, and the garden produced potatoes, corn, and many sorts of vegetables. They had a chicken house with 75 to 100 fowls, and they kept a cow. Mr. Harris enlarged the tiny frame house from two rooms to five, adding two bedrooms and a living room.

When Clyde turned five he was enrolled in the first grade of the Milton School, at that time held in a white frame building. Here he attended school until, at the age of twelve, he graduated from the eighth grade. One of the principal skills he acquired was fist fighting. Clyde was small for his age, and just for amusement at recess time some of the older boys picked on him.

"Clyde called you a nut," or "Clyde said you're a sap," one of them would tell another boy. And that fellow would drag Clyde behind the school's woodshed and give him a pounding. Clyde, in order to defend himself, gradually learned to be tough and scrappy.

Clyde (center) with two of his boyhood chums.

When not fighting, the kids played "long town," a variety of baseball. After hitting the ball, the batter raced to a base and back, while the fielder tried to hit him, "burn him," with the ball.

Summers and after school hours, Clyde wandered for miles through the woods and hills and along the Walla Walla River. Outdoor living, simple food, and plenty of exercise seemed to agree with him, as he does not remember ever having been sick.

Clyde's earliest business venture began simply enough. He loved to fish, and in those days the state allowed a fellow to hook a limit of seventy-five a day. The boy tried selling his surplus fish —mostly trout six to eight inches long—and found a ready market for them in town. His customers demanded that he first clean the trout; then they paid him one cent per fish! He worked up a list of regular customers who would call to him, "When are you going to bring me some more nice fish?"

With this substantial income of a penny a fish, Clyde began to buy his own overalls, shirts, shoes, and hats. After he turned ten the boy never again asked his parents for clothes; he bought his own.

Soon the boy found other jobs—running errands, picking fruit, and turning the freezer handle to make ice cream in stores. In the summer he made additional money selling fruit to passengers on the trains passing through town. The trains stopped for ten or fifteen minutes, which gave him time to hurry along beside them, handing whatever fruit was in season—pears, peaches, apples, apricots, plums, or prunes—to customers leaning from the windows.

By the time he turned thirteen, Clyde found himself meditating more and more on the mysteries of economics and high finance. He had observed that some people in the world comprised the "haves," with money, toys, even bicycles, and others —the Harris family for example—the "have-nots." And he seemed to be discovering, at least in a small way, methods by which members of the latter group could join the former. Already the members of his family, and the neighbors as well, had come to regard him as a businessman, junior edition. When they came home for a visit, his older brothers, some of whom had married and left home by then, would bestow upon Claude or Hazel a dime or a quarter, and sometimes a dollar. But never Clyde; why should they give Clyde money when he was busy cornering his own capital gains in tidy little hunks? The young merchant felt a tinge of resentment at being thus disinherited by his own flesh and blood, but he had to admit that he could not qualify for his brothers' handouts on a basis of need.

When not busy negotiating with apples or apricots, the busy youngster spent his time reading. A pal had introduced him to a series of novels about Diamond Dick, a Western gun artist whose vocation was to combat Hawkeye, an Indian, and heroically slaughter additional thieving, bloodthirsty redskins by the gross. Some nights Clyde would feast his brain on flying fists in bar-rooms, zinging bullets, and bloodied hatchets till he felt goose-pimply about the scalp. Still he read on, fascinated, almost till dawn and time to be up and doing in the business world.

After three years of almost fanatical dedication to Diamond Dick, Clyde happened to read an article in the *Saturday Evening Post*, written by one of America's industrial giants—he cannot remember which. One piece of advice hit him with force: "Do not read anything you do not wish to remember, for by doing so you are training your mind to forget. Then, when you read something you want to remember, you cannot."

"The man is right," Clyde told himself. With great effort he made the decision to leave Diamond Dick and Hawkeye in the sagebrush and cactus to shoot it out for themselves. And the boy never again read a novel or an untrue story of any kind.

Business ventures of many kinds beckoned to the farm youth. People bought flowers. Why not raise and sell them? He boxed up his flowers and sold them in Walla Walla and other towns. He also saved a little from his earnings each month, and by the time he turned eighteen he had begun to buy and improve small pieces of land. Walla Walla Valley orchard land was selling for $200 to $300 an acre. He bought a quarter or half acre at a time, improved it, and sold it at a small profit.

More and more, as Clyde neared the age of twenty, he pondered what his lifework should be. He would reflect on the adults he knew, making a mental list of them, what each did for a living and what kind of income he appeared to make. Half deciding on one occupation, he would back away from it and investigate another.

"I have a few hundred dollars in the bank," he mused. "Should I be a barber? The barbers I know seem to be supporting themselves at least. But what barber has anything in life worth having?

"A confectionery store? Who around here has made a great thing out of that business?

"How about a shoe store?" he asked himself. "I think I would like that, but where does it lead? Same for a drugstore, and I haven't the money to invest. A butcher shop? Mother wouldn't like that. She says it's a cruel, bloody business to spend your life executing defenseless cattle. Guess I'll have to mark that one off.

"A card room? A pool hall? Mother wouldn't like those, either. Nor would I, for that matter. The florist business—I know how to raise and sell flowers. But could I ever be really prosperous as a florist?

"Farming? I like farming, because a farmer can grow as big as he likes if he manages things right. But to get into the farming business takes money for land, buildings, horses, and equipment, far more than I have saved."

In all his mental meanderings, he kept two considerations in view. First, as a budding businessman, he wanted an industry with an open end—something with no upper limit. "Maybe," he mused, "I'm not smart enough to make a big business out of a small one, but at least I want to get into something with no blind alleys, no shackles to success. I may be a failure, but if I am, I want to find it out early in life. Then I can still go to work for the other fellow and be satisfied with that."

His other requirement was that, out of consideration for his mother's religion, he wanted to avoid getting into any line of work that would oblige him to labor on Saturdays, as he expected to be an Adventist someday. Some years before, his mother had taken in washing from a Seventh-day Adventist family by the name of Miller. She had become acquainted with the tenets of that faith, and thereafter regarded Saturday as holy time, not to be used in secular work or play. She had joined the eighty-member church in Milton, the denomination's first in the state of Oregon. She attended services in the little frame church there when health, weather, and the state of clothing permitted.

Mrs. Harris's children felt her devout Christian influence and respected her principles, but with the exception of Mattie they did not attend church with her, partly for lack of proper church attire. Father Harris professed a degree of interest in his wife's religion, but made no special effort to practice it. Though Clyde had never adopted his mother's faith as his own, he felt strangely attracted to it. He intended to join it someday.

Trying to decide what to do with his life, for the time being he worked a five-acre fruit farm, still casting about for something more exciting to do. Eventually he took time out for a vacation, planning to go fishing with a friend, I. H. Taylor. Someone recommended a hotel in the town of Cove where they could stay overnight and leave for the Wallowa mountains the next morning. Arriving in town they learned that the hotel had closed just a week before. But a young boy directed them to a Mrs. Long who lived in a white house and sometimes put up travelers for the night. Clyde and his friend picked up their suitcases and walked four or five blocks up the street. There they saw a white house with a lady busily working in the front yard.

"Are you Mrs. Long?" Clyde asked.

"No, I am not Mrs. Long."

"Well, the hotel is closed, so we are looking for Mrs. Long, who sometimes rents rooms."

"I am not Mrs. Long. I am Mrs. Reese. But I have a room for you if you want it."

Mrs. Reese showed them into the living room, remarking that her husband would be home soon.

When Mr. Reese came in, he and Clyde began to discuss fruit. The conversation lasted all evening.

"Harris, do you know anything about the fruit business?" asked Reese.

"Yes, quite a lot," admitted Harris.

"Apples?"

"Yes, and berries, peaches, prunes, plums, cherries—"

"Have you raised them?"

"Yes, and bought and boxed and sold."

"Say, I had a man working for me, but he took sick today and went home. Can't you come down tomorrow and help me·a few days? You are just on a fishing trip and you can put that off. I need you badly."

After they had talked some more, Clyde agreed to take the job, and Taylor had to take his vacation alone.

Since the other man never came back, Clyde stayed on for weeks. Then one day Reese's boss, Mr. D. M. Clark, the owner of the business, called up: "Harris, Reese has got sick and he can't come to work this morning. You can run this, can't you, till he gets back?"

Clyde guessed he could.

This was berry season, and Harris kept busy buying berries, boxing them, and shipping them out. One of his duties was to purchase boxes at a factory housed in a shed about seventy-five yards away. He asked the manager, named Al, "How's the box business?"

"Not bad. Not bad at all. I'm making a little money."

Clyde and the box tycoon became good friends and hobnobbed around town with each other after working hours. One day to Clyde's surprise his friend boasted, "I've made $4,000 in this business this summer."

"That's an industry worth looking into," Clyde said to himself. "I'll file that one away for further reference."

When Clyde finished working for Mr. Clark, he returned home; and that fall he got a job in Round Valley packing apples. He had secured a contract and hired his brothers C. B. and Darrell to work for him. As they packed apples in boxes, they talked about boxes.

"I don't see why we couldn't turn up some profits in Milton by making boxes," he ventured. "Maybe put up a little factory and see what we can do."

"Maybe we could," allowed Darrell and C. B.

Clyde picked up one of the boxes they were using. "Look at this rough thing," he said. "It looks like it was made of boards from an old barn. We ought to be able to make better boxes than this one."

"I reckon we could," agreed C. B.

By the time Clyde Harris reached the age of twenty, he had already succeeded in a number of small business ventures.

Lumber, Saws, and Fruit Boxes

The apple-packing job lasted almost until Christmas, 1912, at which time Clyde and his brother had decided to go into the box business.

The following Sunday, Clyde, Darrell, and C. B. hired a team and livery rig and drove over to Cove, about fifteen miles away. First they talked with their friend at the box factory, then they consulted the local banker.

"We are from Milton, and we're thinking of going into the box-making business," Clyde told him. "Al says it's a good way to make a living, and he's made $4,000. Do you think he really has?"

"He's a good man," the banker assured them, "and I don't think he's telling you a tall one. He's been doing a good business too."

He declined to be more specific, but this report further convinced the Harris brothers that they, too, belonged in the fruit-box business. They returned to Milton and looked up their father, who was then managing a ranch some miles away on the Walla Walla River. Father Harris got so interested in the box idea that he moved back to Milton, anxious to work with them.

21

Clyde's box-making friend in Cove had told him he would need $1,000 to start a factory, and gave him a list of machinery he would need. However, Clyde soon discovered that the figure was more like $3,500. None of the Harrises knew a thing about box factories or sawmills. But a machinery salesman told them they would need a cutoff saw, a resaw, a ripsaw, and an edger, and they bought these machines.

Clyde, his father, and his brother C. B. borrowed $3,000 of the needed funds from Higby Harris, Clyde's uncle. As security, they mortgaged the Harris home, plus the factory building and equipment. They erected a humble building between Milton and Freewater. The obliging city manager of Milton, a Mr. Coyle, visited them daily, giving instructions as to how to proceed with the carpentry, wiring, and other details. Besides being city manager, Coyle was an electrician and ran the city power plant. He assured the Harrises they were doing a good job of construction.

When they got the building up, but before the machinery arrived, they found they had planned to place the machinery all wrong, so they had to change the floor plan. Coyle showed them how to start the machines, and they were ready to do business as the Milton Box Company.

This was in the spring of 1913. Clyde was twenty-three; his brother, thirty-four. Clyde was manager and operator and C. B. also a manager, and the saw filer. They hired a twelve-year-old boy as a helper, paying him ten cents an hour.

They had bought a carload of lumber from a sawmill in Seattle, and this they sawed up and made into boxes. They managed to sell the boxes, but while selling them they had no money with which to buy more lumber to keep the factory going. Having borrowed all they could to start the factory, they found it difficult to finance another carload of lumber. Without wasting too many days, they were learning that to run a business one needs working capital as well as men, material, and machines.

Somehow they squeaked along, ordering one carload of lumber at a time and hoping to sell enough boxes and collect for them and order more lumber before their saws whined to a halt.

Bankers, predicting that the business would fail, refused to lend them money. Some prophesied failure within three weeks, and one gave them as long as six months. These were local businessmen, and they knew. They said the place to make boxes was over on the Oregon coast, where boxes could be made of odds and ends from the sawmills. A box factory could never succeed in the Walla Walla Valley.

Then help came. A Mr. Robinson, a broker in Walla Walla from whom they had bought some lumber, came over one day and asked them, "Could you use a million feet of this lumber like you've been buying?"

"Maybe," said Clyde, surprised at the offer, but not expecting a miracle. "We could use it over a period of time, but we couldn't pay for it until sold. We couldn't even think about it."

"If we could get you a million feet of lumber, could you use that much?" Robinson persisted.

"We couldn't pay for it until we sold the boxes. I'll talk it over with my brother."

"If we ship you the wood, can you pay the freight on it?"

"Yes. We would try to get enough money to pay the freight."

The lumber came, and this was just the break they needed. Who ever heard of a couple of young fellows in a new business about which they knew almost nothing, getting credit like that? It was not only unusual; it was unbelievable! It took all the Harrises two or three weeks just to unload it. What a secure, comfortable feeling to have mountains of lumber stacked along the railroad tracks and all around the factory! The $2,500 freight bill almost crushed them, but somehow they got it paid off.

Raw material they now had, but buyers kept giving them trouble. Thus far most of their customers, expecting the Milton Box Company to fail any moment, took the bulk of their business elsewhere. One buyer, they learned, had stated, "I will not buy from them, because the more I buy the more money they will lose." The speaker was the biggest box purchaser in Walla Walla Valley. Like the others, this man would buy a small number of boxes from the Harrises when he could get them cheaper or when he needed a few items urgently, but his big orders went to their competitors.

The Milton Box Company was still afloat, just barely, at the end of 1913. They had done a gross business of $13,000 and even turned up a small profit. Clyde and his brother, as their full year's salary, each drew $225 from the profits. Then they closed down the operation and got jobs elsewhere for the winter.

The second year the enterprise limped along about the same as the first year, making a little under $1,000 net. At this time Clyde's father sold his interest in the business to his oldest son George. George later sold his interest, leaving Clyde and C. B. (Clarence Burdette, or "Dette") as sole owners.

In February, 1914, Clyde turned his thoughts briefly from lumber, saws, and fruit boxes to a project of a different kind. He met someone he described as "a nice little girl of seventeen" by the name of Mary Coe. Mary came from a large family living near Milton, but somehow their paths had never crossed until then. Six months later they were married by a local Protestant minister.

On a Sunday a few weeks afterward, Mary announced, "Well, we ought to go to church today."

"If I had been going to church, I'd have went yesterday," Clyde replied.

"What do you mean, you'd have gone to church yesterday?" demanded the bride, shocked at his sudden piety. "You don't mean you would go to the *Adventist* church?"

"Yes, I mean I would have went to the Adventist church."

"Why didn't you tell me that before we were married? I would never have married you!"

In the weeks that followed they consulted with the ministers of both her church and his, and five months later Mary and Clyde both joined the Seventh-day Adventist Church.

Left: Mary Coe, at the age of twelve, posed with younger brother Harold, a lad of nine.

Mary Coe as a teen-age graduate. In February, 1914, Clyde Harris met Mary, "a nice little girl of seventeen." Six months later the couple were married.

Upon declaring himself a practicing Christian, Harris decided to settle some old debts. As a youngster, several times he had employed sticky fingers in the service of his urge to own things. Now he made a list of each petty theft he could remember, visited each wronged person, and paid him back. Most of the items were small, all but one.

Four or five years before, he and two other fellows had swiped a barrel of whiskey, more as a prank than anything else. The barrel lay in an empty store building in Milton. Past midnight the three teen-agers opened the door by sticking a knife between the door and the jamb, easily opening the lock. They rolled out the barrel, loaded it into a wagon, and hid it in a barn belonging to one of the three.

A little later the barrel was found to be empty. Clyde suspected that the fellow in whose barn it was stored had drained the barrel's contents into other containers and sold it to thirsty loggers, but he never knew for sure.

Now Clyde went to the original owner and asked him, "Do you remember that barrel of whiskey you lost?"

"Yes."

"You laid it onto somebody else, did you?"

"Yes."

"Well, he wasn't the man that stole it. I with two other boys took that whiskey from you, and I'm here to make it right. Now, I'll tell what I'll do. There was three of us that stole it. I won't tell you who the other two boys were. I'll pay you one third of the price of that whiskey, if that satisfies you. If not, if you insist, I'll pay you for all of it. If that don't satisfy you, I'll pay for all of it with interest from the time we took it."

"That will be all right, to pay it in full with interest."

Clyde wrote a check for $175 and handed it to him. "Now we're square, aren't we?"

"I reckon so," the man agreed.

That year Clyde had drawn exactly $225 in wages from the Milton Box Company!

When they married, Clyde and Mary could afford no honey-moon. In fact, in view of the teetering finances at the Milton Box Company, they could not afford to rent a house. They fixed up a ten-by-twelve-foot tent as comfortably as possible and moved in. The tent stood near the factory and close to the river from which they drew their water for drinking and housekeeping. But they managed to stay rather happy in this cozy dwelling with its big wood-burning cookstove to heat the bedroom-kitchen-living room. The greatest inconvenience was the intense cold air of January and February, which was hard to keep entirely out of the tent.

Clyde found Mary an excellent housekeeper, as her mother had trained her to be. He liked the meals she cooked, the loaves of bread she baked, the spotless home she kept, even if that home was a ten-by-twelve tent. If anything she did bothered him, it was that she kept things a little too clean and orderly for a man so recently a bachelor.

They allowed themselves one pound of butter a week. Flour was cheap—about sixty cents for a fifty-pound sack. Mary made her own clothes, even her hats. After over a year living in the tent, Clyde found a house they could afford to rent, and from then on he and Mary enjoyed more luxurious living—for $8 a month.

Clyde and Mary, as new members of the Adventist Church, had still more adjustments to make. Three of Clyde's brothers had also joined the church at about the same time, and Clyde told them, "One of these days they're going to call on us to offer prayer, or dismiss the church meeting, or something."

"Oh, no," one of them objected. "They wouldn't do that."

"If they did," said Clyde, "I wouldn't know what to do."

Sure enough, a week or two later Clyde was asked to say a public prayer, which he stumbled through with considerable embarrassment.

Soon they put Clyde to work as a deacon, and made him teacher of a Sabbath School [equivalent to Sunday School]

Six Harris boys. Left to right: C. B. (Burdette), Darrell, Jim,

Claude, Clyde, and George, as they appeared about 1912.

class. To no avail were his arguments that he had never read the Bible, that he didn't know the books of the Bible, that he couldn't pronounce the names. They gave him a class of old people in their seventies, all devout Bible students, to teach.

Clyde later reminisced, "That church didn't give us any time to get lazy or lose interest. They kept us too busy. And that class of old people—I didn't realize it at the time, but they were teaching me instead of me teaching them. The class was determined to make a good teacher out of me if they could. They handled me just about right to get a lot of work out of me, and they made a better man out of me. God was getting me ready to live like I ought to live, and to run my business the way it ought to be run."

Mary had made herself a hat with a spectacular feather on it, about ten inches long. She wore it to church a few times, where she was Sabbath School secretary. After Sabbath School one day, one blunt "sister" in the church came up to her and ordered, "You've got to take that feather off your hat."

"What do you mean?"

"That feather has got to go."

"Why?"

"In our church we don't indulge in worldly display."

"Well, you show me where the Bible says I've got to take it off, and I'll take it off."

That ended the conversation, but Mary decided to take the feather off the hat. If that was part of being a good church member, she wanted to be one, even if it cost the sacrifice of a cherished feather.

The third year and the following, the plant operated with increasing success, and the brothers had to add to their building and machinery. In its February 25, 1916, number the Milton *Eagle* ran the following news items:

BOX FACTORY WILL BEGIN OPERATIONS NEXT MONDAY

Operations will begin at the Milton box factory for the season next Monday, when work will commence on an order for two carloads of lettuce boxes for the greenhouse at Walla Walla River. As soon as this order is completed, sawing of cherry and berry crates will be taken up.

Last season the local plant used about a million and a half feet of lumber, and expect to use fully a third more than this during the season of 1916. They have purchased a sawmill at Wahkiacus, Washington, which is in charge of Dette Harris, one of the company, and lumber will be shipped directly from the mill to Milton. From eight men to thirty will be used in the factory this summer.

In 1924 the plant caught fire and burned to the ground. With some difficulty the Harrises secured financing and rebuilt immediately. Fortunately they had lost only their ramshackle building, not the stockpile of lumber as well.

By the end of the twenties the Milton Box Company had a hundred employees and shipped boxes all over the United States, grossing over $300,000 a year. From the beginning they plowed all possible earnings back into the company, enlarging and improving the plant yearly.

When the great depression of the thirties came, it hit the Milton Box Company hard, threatening to shake down in a few months everything its owners had built up with years of hard work. They had a quarter million dollars in credits, but they owed a good deal of money to banks and finance companies which they could not pay, simply because their debtors could not pay them. In 1932 their bank in Portland urgently requested them to settle a $10,000 account, promising to make the money available again when they got the factory going at capacity in the spring. But the bank changed managers, and when Clyde requested the $10,000 back, the new manager reneged. "We can let you have only $1,000," he told Harris.

Clyde told him he couldn't accept the $1,000, but he would find some way to operate anyway.

The bank manager wished him good luck.

Clyde and his brother decided on three emergency measures: First, they put all their personal funds and securities into the business. Second, they found it necessary to reduce wages slightly. And third, for 40 percent of all salaries, they issued scrip in lieu of cash. The employees knew the company was in trouble and accepted the scrip rather than lose their jobs. They could take the scrip to local stores and get paid in goods with it, or take it to certain persons who would cash it after discounting it. The scrip, a form of note, bore 5 percent interest. All scrip came due for payment six months after issue, and the company never failed to redeem it when it came due. The businessmen of the community demonstrated considerable faith in the Milton Box Company in receiving these company notes in place of cash.

Looking back on the depression days, Clyde later recollected, "In financing our business in 1932 to 1934, we owed the banks and financing houses a lot of money, and we couldn't pay them. I didn't know whether I could stand it or not. When I went to bed at night and knelt down to say my prayers, I wondered if that would be the last time I would be saying or knowing anything. But in the morning after I had had a night's rest, I'd get up feeling better. So I'd go through another few days, and then I'd have one of those spells again when I would be down so low, I wasn't so sure but what I would lose my mind. That went on for some months. But each morning I would get up feeling rested and a little more courageous.

"Day after day when I would receive a telegram I would have to sit down to open it. I was just too weak to stand up. 'More bad news, huh?' I would say to myself, and I would shake like I had the palsy when I opened it. I wondered what could be in it. I tell you this to give you a little idea of what a man goes through in those kind of times when you have one disappointment after another so often that you begin to wonder what's next. But the Lord took care of us. He gave us health, which we are very thankful for."

When crises seemed about to overwhelm him, Harris turned to prayer and Bible study for strength. "I always followed the principle," he says, "'If any of you lack wisdom, let him ask of

God, that giveth to all men liberally.' That's in the book of
James. He has always given this wisdom. Every time we came to
a blank wall, a way would open up.

"Once I told God, 'This is Your work. If You want it to pros-
per, give me health, and I will do my best. If it's Your will that
the business close up, that's all right too.' Then I felt great peace
of mind. I was ready to accept whatever happened."

"I want to say," says Harris, "that most of the bankers were
very nice to us. They gave us time to work things out. They
never bothered us. They just asked us to give them a plan we
could work on, which we did; and then they sat down and waited
for us to fulfill the plan. We did that too. In 1933 they gave us
three years to get our business straightened around. We had it all
paid up in eighteen months, so that everybody was happy. From
that time on our credit became very good. We came out of the
depression quite a little faster than most people. Things were
very cheap, and we were able to buy a large amount of timber
and timber land which in later years became valuable to us."

In 1932, for the first and only time since the business began
in 1912, it lost money. It showed a loss of $6,000 that year as a
result of writing off $75,000 in bad debts. After the crisis had
passed, the Milton Box Company resumed its steady growth.

In 1939 the Federal Government offered timber rights for
thirty years on a huge tract of land—almost fifty square miles—to
the highest bidder. The Harris brothers doubted whether they
should bid on it, but they kept thinking about it.

As the date of the sale drew near, a stranger appeared at
Harris's office one day and asked to see him. Clyde's older sister,
Myrtle, who served as office manager and bookkeeper, received
the visitor and called Clyde. The man wore heavy boots, khaki
pants, a warm coat, and a large white hat. As soon as Clyde
saw him, something told him, "Be careful what you say to this
fellow."

"I am a farmer," the visitor explained, after introducing himself. "I own a piece of land, 160 acres, out in the Ukiah section.

It's surrounded by the land the Government has up for bids."

"Yes."

"Well, the sale is coming up pretty soon, and no doubt you are interested in that sale, so I thought you might be interested in my land."

"No," replied Clyde, "we wouldn't be interested in your land now. The ——— Lumber Company might be interested, though. They will no doubt be the high bidders."

Clyde simply told the man what he honestly thought. He fully believed that his major competitor would bid on the rights and would get them. Acting on his hunch, though, Harris took care not to show any personal interest in the Government timber, though he was still considering bidding on it. What growing lumber and box company would not like to acquire an almost unlimited amount of timber to cut for the next thirty years, at a most reasonable price? About that time a Forest Service representative came in and influenced Harris to bid on it.

Clyde bid $2.16 per thousand board feet on the timber and was the high bidder. The other company came in lower than Clyde's offer and lost out. Bitter over the failure, its officers appealed to the Forest Service to block the Government from granting the concession to Harris. They even took their case to the Secretary of Agriculture in Washington, but failed to upset the decision.

As Clyde later discovered, the "farmer" who visited him was a decoy, a spy from the other lumber mill. He had reported Harris's lack of interest to his company, which then bid low and lost out on the timber rights as a result. Subsequently that company sold out.

Pendleton Beckons

To the Harris brothers there was no other place quite so fine as Milton, Oregon. They had quite naturally chosen Milton as the place to start their business, and it had grown and prospered there for almost three decades. It had become their city's first major industry. Coyle, the friendly city manager, had helped them get started.

The growth of the city had been peaceful, almost idyllic. In a booklet entitled *Early History of the Milton-Freewater Area*, published in 1962 by the Milton *Valley-Herald*, W. S. Caverhill wrote as follows:

Milton-Freewater* has never experienced the exciting stimulation of a "gold rush" that frenzied so many Blue Mountain towns into existence and later left them ghosts of early greatness.

Perhaps the abundant water, the fertile soil, delightful climate, and uninterrupted progress produced a complacency of mind so general among the residents that no thought was given to writing the life story of the area.

---

*In 1889, several families from Milton moved a mile north and founded the town of Freewater. The two towns remained separate until the mid-1950's, when they merged and took the name Milton-Freewater.

To a careful student of social, economic, and civic progress, the fact that Milton-Freewater has arrived from the frontiers of the past without experiencing the turbulence of changing conditions that has plagued the development of other communities is in itself a demand that a history be written, to give credit to the people who did it and tell how it was accomplished.

However, in spite of their love for the town of Milton, toward the end of the thirties the Harris brothers began to contemplate a move. Businessmen in Pendleton, thirty miles to the southwest, took notice of the company's growth potential and invited the Harrises to move their plant to Pendleton. The city offered a thirty-six-acre tract of land, and the businessmen promised $10,000 cash to help pay for the move. After some discussion the Harris brothers accepted the offer. In Pendleton, located thirty miles closer to most of Harris's timber, the company would save sixty miles of driving each time a truck hauled a load of logs in from the woods. Rail service was also more adequate.

After the Harrises started to put up new buildings in Pendleton and close down the Milton operation, city officials in Milton came to them, urging them to stay, even offering them cheaper power. What would it take to get the Harrises not to move, they asked, or at least to keep one plant in Milton?

Clyde replied that their promise had been made to the city of Pendleton, and Pendleton was fulfilling its promises. The Milton Box Company now had no choice but to move.

Construction of the new plant began in December, 1938. It sawed its first log in December, 1939, and opened for business January 1, 1940. The name of the new corporation was Harris Pine Mills. Clyde Harris was president and manager and C. B. Harris secretary. The official opening took place on May 28. In a brochure issued for the occasion, they featured the slogan, "What Pendleton Makes, Makes Pendleton." Some of the facts in the brochure reveal the extent of the plant and its operation:

"The Pendleton plant occupies 36 acres of land. It manufactures approximately 100 different kinds of boxes, all printed with individual stamps, sashes and door stock, and building lumber, including knotty pine.

"The cut of timber at present has reached approximately 6,000,000 feet, of which about one quarter has been remanufactured and shipped to the market as boxes, sash and door cuttings, and lumber. The boxes have gone into Texas and in the Yakima, Walla Walla, and Hood River valleys and the lumber largely into the territory east of Chicago. At present about 4,500,000 feet of lumber are stacked in the yards.

"The plant in Pendleton is one of the most modern of its kind in the West. It is practically under full operation, with approximately 200 men employed in addition to those in the woods operation. The sawmill has a daily capacity of 75,000 feet of lumber and the box factory a daily capacity of 60,000 feet of lumber.

"Each of the four latest type Moore dry kilns has a capacity of 60,000 board feet. Most of the higher class lumber is put through the kilns along with box lumber needed for quick shipment. There is room in the yards for 10,000,000 feet of lumber.

"The garage, 32 by 64 feet, has equipment available for repairing the thirteen trucks, two lumber carriers, and two tractors with bulldozers.

"The entire plant has a complete blower system for eradicating dust, shavings, and sawdust.

"A railroad spur connecting with the Union Pacific main line serves both the log pond and the box factory, with floor-level facilities at the factory."

Two years after the move to Pendleton, Clyde bought out his brother C. B.'s interest and became the sole owner of Harris Pine Mills. C. B., whose health was failing, moved back to Milton and died two years later.

When the industry had gotten on its feet after the move, Harris offered to refund to the city of Pendleton the $10,000 cash the businessmen had given him. He was told that he need not return the money; it was a gift, not a loan. Harris had fulfilled his obligations to the city; no one was dissatisfied. Clyde told the city fathers, he wanted to return the money anyway, so they accepted and used it to improve a city park.

World War II brought a host of new problems to Harris Pine Mills, as it did to other industries of every kind. Shortages of materials and freight cars, price controls, and drafting of skilled help were only a few. But Clyde tackled each problem as it came, often praying for guidance from God. The plant produced day and night throughout the war.

Before the war Harris Pine Mills had accumulated a good supply of such items as nails, wire, saws, hinges, screws, truck tires, and parts for trucks, tractors, and machinery. In fact, so ample were their supplies of these parts that the company was able to operate all through the period when some of the items were unavailable.

When freight cars were in short supply to ship lumber, Clyde succeeded in getting a top priority, since boxes were needed to ship perishable fruit and lumber for the war effort. When the government froze prices on shook (the boards from which boxes are made) for shipping ammunition, Harris was assigned an attractive price. A few months before the freeze, he had raised his prices and in return these prices were assigned him by the Office of Price Administration, commonly known as the O.P.A.

In 1946 the company began to manufacture furniture. As Clyde tells it, "My wife wanted some furniture made of a certain kind, and we couldn't buy it at the store. So she said she would have it made down at our plant. She had some furniture made—bedsteads and chests of drawers, a cabinet or two, a table, and a few chairs. After she got them made, she liked them very much and suggested that we make furniture like it to sell. So we started to make a little furniture.

"We didn't know anything more about the furniture business when we went into it. We didn't even know the different kinds of machines they used in making furniture. Well, we hired a

Clyde and Mary Harris have taken active part in Pendleton's civil and social affairs. In this picture taken in 1950 they wait by the Indian village to ride in the Roundup parade.

young man by the name of Device to come and start us out in it. He had previously managed two furniture factories. He stayed with us a year. At the end of that year we could manufacture furniture. Of course, maybe not as good as he could make it, and not as good as others were making it. But we soon learned, and we improved our furniture every year."

Three years after Harris Pine Mills began to manufacture furniture, they had become the largest maker of unfinished furniture in the world.

Relations between the city fathers of Pendleton, and the Harris Pine Mills, the city's largest industry, remained on a most cordial basis. However, after a decade of growth in that city, clouds began to gather—dense clouds of gray smoke billowing out of the company's stacks. The company was sawing more wood and burning more dust and shavings. The smoke pretty well blanketed the city. People complained, and someone had to do something about it.

The company invited 250 businessmen and civic leaders of Pendleton to a banquet to talk things over. Harris gave a speech in which he discussed the problem frankly.

"We are making a lot of smoke in Pendleton," he said, "more than we had ever thought we would make when we moved here. When we moved to this city we promised you a payroll of $150,-000 a year, which you thought would be very nice. Today we are giving you a payroll of many times that amount. But we are giving you a lot of smoke with it. Now, we don't like this smoke any better than you do. We have tried to eliminate the smoke. We have spent thousands of dollars trying to get rid of it. We are making some progress, and we are not through. We know we haven't got rid of it yet.

"This is what I wanted to talk to you about: We must enlarge our plant. Our business has grown until we must have more capacity. We have been thinking about curtailing our operations in Pendleton and putting part of our plant over on the Columbia River, thus getting rid of the smoke problem in Pendleton. We have been planning and counseling with engineers, and we find it will take about $100,000 to cure the smoke problem. We are not sure that amount will do it.

"Now we are going to leave the decision to you men here in town. You can tell us what to do. We have come to the crossroads in our business. We've got to grow; that is the only alternative we have. You tell us what to do, and we will do it."

Harris sat down.

Mayor Norman Gorfkle stood to his feet and said, "Clyde, we know there is smoke here. We know people are kicking about it. We know that it is a little embarrassing to you. But, you know, we *like* smoke. We ask you to stay right here, smoke and all."

The other businessmen unanimously agreed. Rhapsodized a writer in the Pendleton *East Oregonian*, "I love the smoke from Harris Pine Mills. It smells like crisp dollar bills to me."

So Harris Pine Mills stayed in Pendleton, and the business kept growing. Eventually they almost eliminated the smoke nuisance. There is still a little smoke, but the dirty cinders no more spread over the city.

Through the years Clyde did his best to maintain cordial employee relations. "We find," he says, "that if we pay our men well and treat them fair, we have the best success. We try to treat them all alike."

But there have been incidents. Once a young man came to Harris in the fall. His wife, explained the applicant, needed an operation and the hospital would not take her unless he was assured of a job all winter. Winter was the slack season, and Clyde had no plans to hire new employees in the autumn. But the young man pleaded for help for his sick wife, so Clyde gave him a job. A year or two later this man, influenced by another employee, quit his job and moved away.

Later he had a change of heart. He wrote Clyde a letter, confessing that he had stolen quite a quantity of material from the company and stating that he wanted to replace it.

"We didn't let these incidents bother us too much," recollects Harris. "We tried to put ourselves in the other man's shoes and look at it from his point of view, knowing he worked hard every week and was bound to have discouraging days and times. We tried to give him the benefit of the doubt. Perhaps he didn't really mean all that he said or did."

In 1946 fire struck again, and the sawmill burned down. Harris, in Chicago at the time, learned of the loss by phone. Insurance covered part of the loss, but the company had to spend a part of its $300,000 bank account to rebuild. But they rebuilt better and larger. Later Harris regarded the fire as a blessing.

Restored
to the Lord

By the year 1950, Clyde and Mary Harris found themselves the prosperous owners of the largest industry in Pendleton, and one of the largest in eastern Oregon. As owner and manager, Clyde paid himself a salary of $40,000 a year out of earnings.

Besides the huge plant in Oregon, the Pine Mills had branches in Illinois, Texas, and Virginia. They owned many thousands of acres of forest—enough to supply the huge operation for years. They had machinery to cut the trees down, trim them, and cut them into lengths. They operated seventeen tractors to assemble the logs in the woods and move them to a central point where they could be loaded. They owned a fleet of logging trucks that each hauled 5,000 to 8,000 feet of logs or lumber at a time. They had built roads into the timber, spending as much as $500,000 on a single road. They had acres of stacked logs and lumber and enormous drying kilns. The Pendleton operation occupied forty acres of land and employed 400 people.

Since the early days of struggle, when Clyde and Mary Harris had joined the Milton Seventh-day Adventist Church, they had tried to cooperate with Someone they regarded as an unseen Partner in the business—God. They had given a tenth of all profits, according to the tithing principle followed by Christians of many faiths. They had tried to be fair with their employees and even to go the second mile. Clyde had on occasion hired employees who had little to offer the company, simply because the applicants had a hard-luck story and needed the work. The Harrises had closed the huge operation from sundown Friday till sundown Saturday, refraining from all secular work on the day they held sacred. They regarded themselves not as creators and owners of a wealthy, successful enterprise, but as stewards of a business whose real owner was God, and as recipients of talents God had given them to use in the business world.

What else could God expect of them? Clyde tried to find the answer to this question over and over again as he neared the age of sixty. He talked the matter over with his wife, and the couple, who had no children, thought they should will the business to God for the strengthening of His church when they were gone. Agreeing on this, they made out their will to the General Conference of Seventh-day Adventists.

Was there something more God would have them do? Clyde felt there might be, but for months he tried to dismiss the idea from his mind. His thoughts, as he later described them, went something like this:

"Lord, we are giving it all to You when we die. When we are dead, You can have it. Not now, but a little later. That will make a wonderful gift to You."

Then Clyde seemed to hear God reply, "If you love Me, why wait till you are dead to give it? Why not now?"

Clyde shrugged the thought off impatiently. "Well, I can't do that. It's been my life's work. Besides, nobody else can run it, and that's final."

Again he brushed away the idea, but it did not stay brushed. In his resistence he experienced help. The tempter, he says, whispered, "Take your time. No hurry; think it over. Be careful, now, what you do. This is your entire life's work, and you may need it."

Months went by while Harris hung on to this great industrial plant into which he had poured his life. Then, he says, God whispered again, "Why not give it now?"

At last he discussed his growing convictions with Mary. She, too, felt that such a decision would not be necessary. It would be too great a sacrifice. They were proud of the plant. They had worked so hard!

He talked with some of his closest friends in the church. Some advised him in this vein: "Now, Clyde, I wouldn't do this if I were you. Those preachers can't run this plant. They will lose it all and a lot more money with it. You are doing a good job, and you ought to keep it and operate it."

At last, says Clyde, God won out. He and Mary both agreed that the best is none too good for God. He had given them the industry. He had granted them good health. He had bestowed the wisdom to make the right choices at the right time so that they had prospered beyond their dreams. He had been their Partner; they could trust Him to manage it well. They were getting along in years, and they couldn't take Harris Pine Mills with them. So why not give it back in grateful acknowledgment of His blessings—now, while they still lived?

Together they dedicated Harris Pine Mills to God: Pendleton plant and branch plants, logging trucks, tractors, forest roads, timber, buildings, machinery, and acres of cut logs and drying lumber.

One Sunday morning in the spring of 1952 Clyde summoned the 400 employees to lay aside their tools, shut off their machines, and gather for an announcement. Standing on a platform by the mill pond, his back to the factory, Clyde revealed that he had given the entire $10,000,000 plant to the church. Over their heads fluttered a banner, four feet by twenty-four, reading in black letters, THE GOSPEL TO ALL THE WORLD. He explained simply that "We owe our prosperity to the Lord," for "every time I came to a blank wall the Lord opened an avenue of escape."

Harris Pine Mills from the air, with Umatilla River at lower

left. Foreground: Log decks well stocked for winter sawing.

From then on, he told his employees, they would be working for the church, but he hastened to assure them that, whether Adventist or of some other faith, they were welcome to remain; there would be no discrimination because of religious belief or for any other reason.

As for himself, he said, he expected to "fish and read the Bible," secure in the knowledge that "I have used the talents entrusted to me and have returned them, with interest, into God's work."

Clyde and Mary Harris kept for their own use some cattle, grassland, and timber acreage they could not readily sell.

Previous to this public announcement, Harris had conferred at length with William H. Branson, Adventist world president, and other church leaders, planning for an orderly transfer of ownership and management. Harris had his eyes on a tall, dark-haired young man by the name of Charles J. Nagele, of Portland. Nagele, who served as treasurer of his denomination's administrative headquarters for the Northwest, was a mere thirty-seven years of age. As a youth he had worked for a sawmill belonging to his father, but of course he had had no managerial experience in a competitive industry such as this one. However, on Clyde's recommendation, Nagele was elected vice-president and assistant manager. Harris planned to stay on as manager for two years, until Nagele became thoroughly acquainted with the business.

"I had been serving for several years on a denominational administrative committee," explains Harris. "Nagele was also a member of that committee, and though he didn't know it, I was observing him. I saw his talent for making decisions, and his attitude toward other people. I noticed that he was open-minded; he was not afraid of new ideas. And besides, he was young enough so that he wouldn't be ready to retire by the time he learned to manage the business."

When Nagele arrived in Pendleton, Harris led him on a tour of the sprawling plant. Meeting one of the foremen, Clyde

Charles J. Nagele, who became manager of Harris Pine Mills following the retirement of Clyde Harris, the founder.

would say, "Meet your new manager, Mr. Charles Nagele."
Then he would explain to Nagele that Mr. ——— was foreman of
this department. Then they would be off to the next department.

The next day Harris told Nagele, "You'll never learn if I stay
around to hold your hand," and flew to Alaska for a month's stay
among mountains, forests, and streams he loved.

"I couldn't even remember the names of all the foremen to
whom I had been introduced," recollects Nagele, and adds, "The
biggest joke in eastern Oregon was that a *preacher* was now trying to run a multimillion-dollar lumber, box, and furniture
empire." Bankers, brokers, and merchants from Portland to
Chicago expected the industry to come crashing to the ground
like a ponderosa pine in one of the Harris forests. For a couple
of years after Nagele's arrival, the banks for one reason or
another did not have funds available when Harris Pine Mills
wanted a loan.

It's good to have a laugh once in a while in eastern Oregon
or anywhere else. How droll, after all, to take a parson and try
to make an industrialist out of him. How frightfully funny to
take a gentleman who presumably has spent his life sipping tea
at the Ladies' Aid Society, smiling seraphically as he pronounces
blessings on the babies, and benignly dispensing good advice
from behind a pulpit, and plunge the poor fellow into the merci-
lessly competitive world of big business, then expect him to make
a thundering success out of it!

However, the skeptics erred on three counts: they under-
estimated Nagele, they misjudged Harris, and they failed to do
their homework on the Pine Mills' new owners, the Seventh-
day Adventist Church.

Nagele, though an ordained minister who has often preached
from a pulpit and is happy to acknowledge the fact, is primarily
an administrator and an executive. Before moving to the Northwest he had successfully administered the Paradise Valley Sani-
tarium and Hospital, located in a suburb of San Diego. More
recently he had served as financial administrator for his church

in a five-state area, bearing heavy responsibilities in the management, operation, and building expansion programs of churches, hospitals, high schools, and a college. When *Life* magazine reported that "The Rev. C. J. Nagele . . . has never had any previous business experience," it was handling the facts loosely.

As for Harris, he could hardly have developed the Harris Pine Mills into the industry it became if he had been unable to pick capable men, train them, and let them shoulder responsibility. When he chose his successor he was shrewd enough to know that Nagele could take hold of the business and keep it going.

And finally, the Seventh-day Adventist Church uniquely combines devout evangelical activity with phenomenally sound, feet-on-the-ground managerial and financial organization on a worldwide scale. If one were to gather all the Seventh-day Adventists in the United States and Canada, adults and children, into one place, they would number fewer than the population of Atlanta, Indianapolis, or Portland, Oregon. Yet in North America alone this denomination operates eleven colleges and two universities with an enrollment of 14,500; seventy-eight high schools and 1,000 elementary schools; forty-three hospitals; and five publishing houses with an annual output of $20,000,000. In the United States, Australia, and other countries, Adventists own and operate sizable food processing and manufacturing plants. At the same time this small denomination lavishly exports personnel, including some of its ablest educational and administrative leaders, to less-developed countries of the world where more than one half of the Adventist membership resides. Thus, even though the new owners of Harris Pine Mills had not served their apprenticeship in the logging camp, they were hardly strangers to business management.

After giving Nagele a month to get acquainted with his new job, Harris was back in Pendleton from his Alaskan trip. He introduced Nagele to the furniture marts in Chicago, San Francisco, and other cities, and strolled through the plant and into the ponderosa forests.

Once on a bitter winter day in the forest, Nagele was shivering, blue with cold. Out of years of habit, he still wore a white dress shirt such as he used at the office. In fact, he owned no other kind.

"Is that the only shirt you got?" asked Harris.

"Well, yes—"

The next day Harris bought him two heavy maroon-colored woolen shirts—Pendleton brand, no less. Twenty dollars apiece.

From the start, Nagele had three men who believed in him: W. H. Branson, Clyde Harris, and C. A. Scriven, Adventist church leader in the northwestern states. Branson, the new chairman of the board, reassured Nagele, "Stay with it for five years, young man. If you want out then, we'll see that you get a job as good as the one you left."

Ten years later, Reuben R. Figuhr, who had succeeded Branson as Adventist world leader and Harris Pine Mills board chairman, was talking with him. "Now I've been here for ten years," Nagele offered, "and—"

logs daily. The trucks are driven over 250,000 miles a year.

"Stay with it five more, and then we'll talk about it," insisted Figuhr.

Those five years also have passed. Nagele still runs Harris Pine Mills, and obviously enjoys his job immensely. The "preacher" has made good, and the laughter has long since died down. In 1954 he became executive vice-president, and in 1958, president and chairman of the operating board.

In the fifteen years since the Harrises "restored to the Lord" their business enterprise, it had quadrupled in sales volume. With fifteen branches, 1,200 employees, and 300 salesmen and representatives, the gross business now amounts to over $1,500,-000 a month, servicing 6,000 accounts. Currently business is increasing at a rate of about $1,000,000 a year.

The industry uses 100,000,000 board feet of lumber yearly in all its divisions. As many as fifty truckloads and twenty railroad carloads of logs arrive daily to be cold decked or dumped into the millpond and await their turn at the big bandsaw, after which the lumber will go directly to the dry kilns or spend some time in the forty acres of drying yard. The truck fleet drives over 250,000 miles a year on hundreds of miles of forest roads. Daily $1,500 worth of wood chips, a by-product, are sold to pressed-board or paper manufacturers.

From the time the Mills became the property of the Adventists, the church has neither sought nor received preferential tax exemption of any kind. Denominational leaders felt that it would be unfair to seek financial favors from the Government, thus placing competitors at a disadvantage. Tax exemption for church-owned businesses is a matter of increasing concern to leaders of both religion and business.

The Wall Street Journal for October 29, 1963, published a report under the heading, "Many Religious Groups Reap Tax-free Profits in Commercial Ventures." The article was subtitled "Catholic Groups Make Wine, Own Yankee Stadium Land; Baptists Buy Textile Mill."

The ecclesiastical enterprises are sparking a sizzling new controversy over church-state relations. Critics include businessmen who charge that tax exemptions subsidize church-owned businesses in competition with private enterprise. . . . Dr. Eugene Carson Blake . . . of the United Presbyterian Church . . . prophesies sarcastically that "with reasonably prudent management, the churches ought to be able to control the whole economy of the nation within the predictable future."

The article took notice, however, of certain exceptions—church-owned institutions that willingly pay their full share of taxes:

"The Seventh-day Adventists have paid income taxes on Harris Pine Mills since a member gave them that Oregon property in 1951."

Says Nagele, "Harris Pine has paid tremendous sums to the Government in taxes, but I am sure that the Lord was leading us when we set this company up as a taxable company. We wouldn't change it now if we could."

Pendleton businessmen are well aware of the impact of such an industry on their community, but in the spring of 1962 the company decided to dramatize the fact. From the Federal Reserve Bank in San Francisco they obtained $100,000 in $2 bills, and paid their payroll and all local accounts in the eccentric currency. This included the month's electric bill of $7,000. The local supermarkets soon had sacks full of the bills, and practically every business in town gazed upon more portraits of Thomas Jefferson than they had seen since the dawn of time. The super-abundance of the exotic currency in Pendleton cash registers resembled a plague of grasshoppers in North Dakota, or the scourge of frogs in Pharaoh's Egypt. The bills showed up in quantities in Milton-Freewater, Walla Walla, and other nearby towns. Only after six weeks had most of the pestiferous wampum trickled out of town and back to the Federal Reserve.

But the impact of Harris Pine Mills does not stop with Pendleton and vicinity. Long before Clyde and Mary Harris signed over their industry to the church, they had taken a special interest in providing struggling students with employment so that they might work their way through college. With continuing growth in recent years, this program has been stepped up until today 1,200 students in college and secondary school earn a substantial part of their school expenses working for Harris Pine Mills. Numbers of these students attend Walla Walla College, in College Place, Washington, forty-two miles from Pendleton. The Mills have deliberately located most of their fifteen branch factories near other Adventist schools, where as many students as possible can be employed. Branches are now located in Oregon, Washington, California, Colorado, Illinois, Wisconsin, Indiana, Pennsylvania, New Jersey, Georgia, Texas, and Massachusetts.

The company maintains showrooms in Seattle, San Francisco, Chicago, and New York. A strong management training program is carried on at the Pendleton home office and plant, to staff its far-flung empire.

The Pine Mills have been able to take over six struggling

Twelve hundred students earn a substantial part of their secondary-school and college expenses working at the Mills.

wood industries run by secondary schools and make the businesses pay. One such school industry had lost as much as $100,-000 a year. The board urged Harris Pine Mills to take over the operation, and after due consideration this was done.

Furniture production now acounts for 80 percent of the entire business, and lumber and fruit boxes only 20 percent; in recent years paper and plastic boxes have given wood boxes heavy competition, thus the shift in emphasis. The redwood products division, with factories in Watsonville, California, Cicero, Indiana, and Columbus, Wisconsin, is now the world's largest producer of redwood patio furniture. It uses 30,000,000 feet of redwood a year. The new hardwood division at Gaston, Oregon, and Auburn, Washington, turns out furniture of maple and alder.

Is Harris Pine Mills strictly impartial in its employment policies?

"In view of the fact that the Mills are denominationally owned," explains Nagele, "we are extra careful to treat Adventist and non-Adventist alike. Applicants for employment are never asked concerning their beliefs, nor is their race taken into account."

Why, then, the large proportion of Seventh-day Adventists throughout the organization?

"Many Seventh-day Adventists have problems with their jobs because of their observance of the seventh-day Sabbath," says Nagele. "So they tend to gravitate to jobs where they will never be asked to work on their Sabbath. Adventists from all over the country come here for this reason. We have quite a number from Southern states, for instance. Also, certain people simply don't feel comfortable here. The typical lumberjack, for example, hates to work for a company where he feels out of place if he cusses, or where the strongest thing he can find to drink in the woods is a can of 7-Up."

"What about your branches located by Adventist schools?"

"Naturally the great majority of the students are Adventists.

But our denominational schools also enroll young people from other denominations."

"What does the Department of Labor say?"

"They have investigated our employment policies, and tell us they are satisfied we are not practicing discrimination."

Does employment of student labor give the Pine Mills a jump on their competitors?

To begin with, Harris Pine Mills does not employ students exclusively by any means. Hundreds of adults make up the "hard core" of the working force. As for the students, "We could never employ so many of them without the help of God," says Nagele. "We have to build these students' work program to fit in and around their class schedules. And few businesses would even try to employ so large a number of constantly changing laborers, training in a new, unseasoned group of young people each year. It is not easy or cheap to employ hundreds of students, but we do it because this is one of the aims of the company and its owners."

Still, the students aren't doing badly, thank you. So far none of the branches has failed to make a profit in any year since it was opened. The company has a triple-A credit rating, and if the Mills needed credits its manager could borrow an amount into seven figures by lifting his office phone and dialing a bank.

A few die-hard skeptics still circulate the rumor that Clyde Harris stands just offstage manipulating the ropes; otherwise the "preachers" in charge would lead the company swiftly down the road of decline and ruin. The truth is that, though Harris is still a member of the board, he is definitely retired from the business and has been for several years. He can relax in his cabin by the lake or do whatever he chooses, leaving the cares of management to young men like Nagele, Charles Fry, Norman Thorgerson, Ernest Porter, and Walter Bain, the corporate officers, who are so successfully running the industry. "If a truck should run over both Harris and me the same day," says Nagele, "Harris Pine Mills would continue to operate and grow as it has in the past."

In 1963 and into 1964 the Harrises made a round-the-world tour, flying to Hawaii, the Orient, Middle East, and Europe.

When the Harrises signed over their Mills to the Adventist Church in 1951, they kept some of their lesser possessions—cattle, grasslands, and timber. By 1964 these properties had multiplied and appreciated greatly, and the Harrises decided the time had come to restore more property to the Lord. This time the gift included 5,000 head of cattle and 30,000 acres of land.

Their last gift has yet to be given. Harris has instructed Nagele, "If anything happens to us, everything is for the Lord," and wills read accordingly. Even his personal clothing is to go to the church's Dorcas-Welfare Society, the organization that collects, repairs, and distributes food, clothing, and bedding to the needy at home and abroad.

Late in 1963 and into 1964, Clyde and Mary Harris embarked on a world tour. First they flew to Hawaii, then Japan, Korea, the Philippines, Singapore, India, Pakistan, Iran, Iraq, Lebanon, Greece, Turkey, Spain, France, England, and back to the United States. In Poona, India, Clyde addressed a church gathering of 1,500 people. They visited mission stations that their large gift to the church had helped to establish and maintain. They met foreign missionaries—ministers, doctors, nurses, teachers—who had worked their way through college thanks to the Pine Mills.

Have Clyde and Mary Harris ever had second thoughts about giving away what they devoted their life to acquiring?

"We are very happy we made the decision to give our plant to the Lord when we did," says Clyde. "We wouldn't have it any other way. We look forward to the time when we can meet our Saviour and know that we helped with what we had to further the message of God on this earth. When we die, our will gives everything we have to Him, which we are very happy for.

"We had difficulties, plenty of them. But God led us and saw us through them. He didn't give us success all at once, but helped us along from day to day and month to month. He didn't let us make too much money at one time, and He didn't let it get too hard. He had us hemmed in. He had a top line to keep us from getting too proud and taking off on our own, trying to get along without Him. And He didn't let it get so bad that we got discouraged and quit."

Since retirement the Harrises have enjoyed travel, photography, and relaxation among the mountains, streams, and forests. They own a comfortable vacation home by a lake in the Wallowa Mountains. And of course, from their home on a slope overlooking the city of Pendleton, they can see the Mills. When the wind is right, they can smell the faint, fragrant odor of burning pine chips.

What, in Harris's view, are the secrets of getting ahead in business?

Clyde answers modestly, "To succeed today, starting with nothing, is much harder than when I started with nothing. In those days properties were not worth very much. As a rule, every year they are worth more. It takes a bigger investment to get started today.

"One rule is never to draw any more money out of a business than you have to. Spend as little as you can until the enterprise is prosperous enough to take out profits.

"You must give all your time to a business, day and night. Think about it, and read everything you can find on it.

"My plan has always been mass production at a very narrow margin; not to raise prices to make more money, but to manufacture and sell a larger volume of goods to make more money. We have been successful, I believe, for that reason.

"Also, we don't use liquor, tobacco, or narcotics. We try to live healthfully so that we can think clearly and quickly.

"God has told us that under certain conditions He would bless us. We have tried to do our part, probably not as well as we ought to. Our purpose has been to be an asset to the nation and to serve God, and He has blessed us all these years."

*   *   *   *   *

In the Oregon woods another giant ponderosa destined for Harris Pine Mills crashes to the ground. And the echo of the sound is heard to the remotest corner of the globe, because a man and his wife took their very best and gave it back to God.

From Logs Into Furniture
A Busy Factory in Operation

Opposite page: Nerve center for the far-flung Harris Pine Mills operations is the home office at Pendleton, Oregon. Above: Jammer tips load of logs from truck into log pond.

HOWDYSHELL

Above: A jammer, or crane, hoists logs onto the winter log deck. **Opposite page:** Another view of jammer in action.

A chain saw cuts a floating log to manageable lengths preparatory to debarking and cutting on the giant bandsaw.

Opposite page: The pond man rides the rolling, bobbing logs as he sorts species and brings them in for sawing.

Opposite: A workman poles logs toward debarker. Above:
Water under great pressure removes the bark from logs.

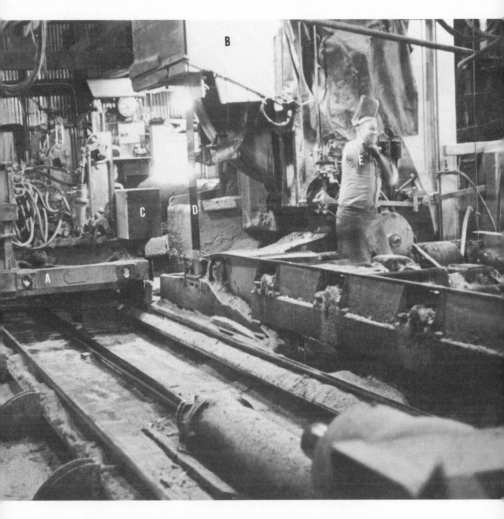

Opposite: Workman with peavey pushes logs toward elevator chain which raises them into position for sawing. Above: Bandsaw rapidly cuts logs into heavy boards. A, carriage; B, head rig; C, log; D, bandsaw blade; E, tail sawyer.

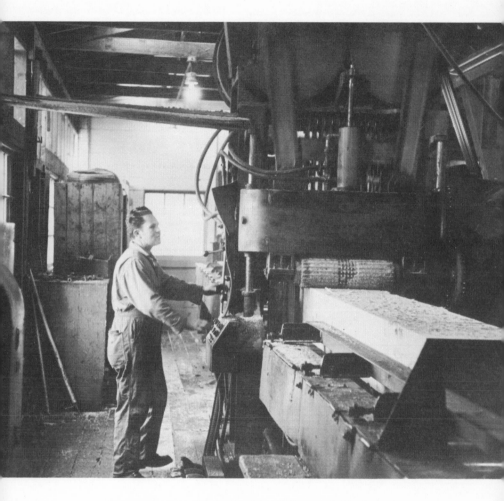

The gang mill, with its battery of giant saw blades,
cuts the heavy slabs of timber into rough boards.

Diesel fork lift stacks lumber in the yard for air drying.

The straddle carrier, or "straddlebug," takes away a load of lumber from the planer.

Employee stickers green lumber to go into the dry kilns. In this case they're 2 x 10's.

Lumber is loaded into a railroad freight car for shipment.

Left: Grease gun in hand, a workman lubricates cutoff saw.

With this bank of cutoff saws the operators grade and sort lumber, cutting to length and discarding defective parts.

Cutoff saw operators process thousands of feet of lumber daily.

Above: At pickup belt, employees remove stock which has been cut to length. Right: Another view of the pickup belt.

At the bank of line rips, boards are cut to width, using line from shadow cast by overhead lights as cutting guide.

A student employee earns her
school expenses by operating
one of the line-rip machines.

In an operation called tailing the pony planer, a workman stacks glued boards after the planing.

Another student worker operating the line rip.

PART DETAIL NUMBERS (5 Digit System)

SAMPLE: **3F25C**

Material	Description	Length	Detail
MAHOGANY 1 green	A—Back	1 1	A
CLEAR PINE 2 white	B—Base		B
	C—Cleat		C—COMMON
KP PINE 3 goldenrod	D—Door	2 2	D
	E—End		E
	F—Front	3 3	F
CLEAR SCARF 4 yellow	G—Guide		G
	H—Shelf, Horizontal	4 4	H
KP SCARF 5 pink	L—Leg		J K
	P—Post, Partition, Divider	5 5	L—LEFT
BLUE 6 blue	Q—Panels, Doors		M N
	R—Rail, Spacer, Brace	6 6	O Q
7	S—Side		R—RIGHT
	T—Top	7 7	S—SPECIAL
8	U—Bottom, Understructure	8 8	T—TRIPLE DOOR DADO
	V—Corner Blocks		U V
9	X—Trim	9 9	W
	Z—Miscellaneous		X—MULTIPLE
			Y—2nd MULTIPLE
0		0 0	Z

This chart, which appears complicated to the uninitiated but is in reality quite simple, is a key that identifies furniture parts by number.

In an operation known as "tailing the tenoner," two girls remove furniture parts from the machine. The maze of tubes takes away sawdust.

Six identical furniture pieces are cut on the bandsaw.

◀ A craftsman sets up a molder, a machine which makes dadoes, grooves, and beveled edges for producing attractive furniture.

Drawer fronts, nearing completion, are fed into the molder. ▶

◀ Another craftsman keeps busy shaping the legs for furniture.

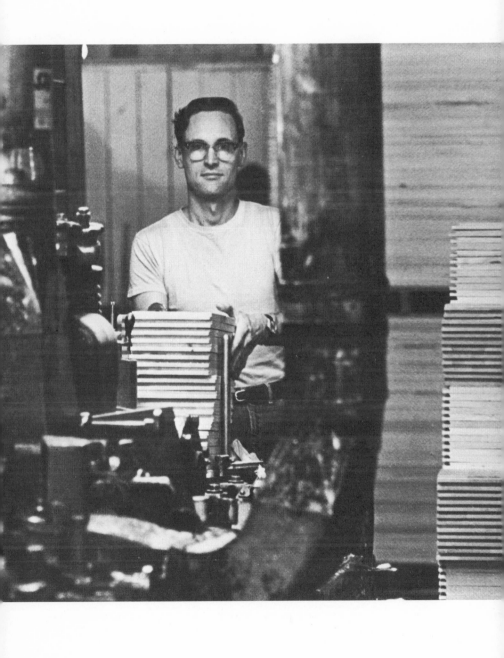

Above: A workman shapes contoured ends of a "deacon's bench." Opposite page, above: Drawer fronts are fed into a belt sander. Below: Molder disgorges furniture parts onto revolving table, ready for stacking.

Above: A workman incarcerates himself behind antique-style chair as he assembles it. Opposite: The chair nears completion as he taps it together with a mallet.

The automatic nailer speeds assembly of drawers for desks and dressers.
This machine accelerates production by driving twelve nails at one time.

With airgun stapler, a workman rapidly attaches the back to a chest.

Final assembly completed, desks are packed for shipment to customers of Harris Pine Mills, the largest producer of pine and redwood furniture.